ANGELS IN SEVEN

ANGELS IN SEVEN

MICHAEL MILLER

MOON TIDE PRESS

Irvine, California

2016

Copyright © 2016 by Michael Miller.
All rights reserved.

No part of this book may be used or reproduced in any manner whatsoever without written permission except in the case of brief quotations embodied in critical articles and reviews.

For information or inquiries, email sedavis@uci.edu.

Miller, Michael, 1979-
Angels in Seven / Michael Miller – 1st ed.

ISBN 13: 978-0-9974837-0-3
ISBN 10: 0-9974837-0-3

Moon Tide Press
Irvine, California
www.moontidepress.com

Cover design by Michael Miller
Back cover and interior design by Michael Wada
First edition / Printed in the United States of America

The makers of this book wish to thank all of those who have helped to keep Moon Tide Press thriving since its founding in 2006: Lee Mallory, Ricki Mandeville, Zoot Velasco, Mindy Nettifee, John Turi, Michael Wada and all of the wonderful authors, editors, venue hosts, cover artists, patrons and subscribers to whom we owe our utmost gratitude.

For

Peter Srisavasdi

(1944-2016)

Contents

I

The Chicago Window Washer Lets His Soap Paintings Stay	13
Diary: 35th Birthday	15
What We're Sure Of	17
Interview with the Songwriter	20
Arboretum	22
To Rachanee, Laguna Beach, Jan. 1	23
One Word	24
To the Student Still Without a First Draft Tuesday Morning	26
Out of Ideas	28

II

Angels in Seven	33

III

Men at the Hotel Pool	43
Woman Next Door	44
Day After New Year's	45
After His First Surgery	46
Salvaged	48
Ride Home	49
First Condo	50
New Place	51
Our Money's Worth	52

IV

Poems at the Station	57
Departures	59
Park in Reykjavik, Iceland	62
Housewarming, East Los Angeles	65
Bonfire at Cape Cod with Marge Piercy's Workshop	67

Crossing, Harpers Ferry   68
Virginia Museum of Fine Arts   70
Alaska Airlines Nonstop to LAX   72

Acknowledgements   75
About the Author   76

No one is great among us. This is our best joy.

—*Susan Davis*

I

The Chicago Window Washer
Lets His Soap Paintings Stay

If the cable snaps today,
                 his ideas will not go with him.

    This time, he lets the hasty marks dry,
the lines usually swallowed
   by his wavering bucket of water
              now directing the sun's traffic through.

     With his rosary from Mexico in pocket
and Wacker Street below
           gray and sterile as a slab before surgery,

   he fastens his cable each dawn
             and scales the building's silent face.
Invisibility is the gift

     he gives the city,
   his fingers without documents
to be fingers for real

   dragging the blade's bent rubber
         until no trace stays behind.

        On the free days at the museum,
   attended always in his one clean tie,
his eyes check the death dates beside the frames,
          the record of so many cords giving way.

When any body lands,
      what survives the blow at the bottom?

He imagines the flight that follows,
    the dashing of breath and size and debt
       and the sky poised to catch the ideas and name.

        It is the fear of loud voices
     that keeps so much confined,
          so today, he has drawn
               where the yelling boss won't see.

    Before the office with the door shut all summer
and the mouse dangling where the modem sat,
          his Rothko
               cuts the sky in three:

          one layer splotchy,
          one streaked straight
               and pure light
                    sandwiched in the middle.

     On half of the corner office
     that the recession voided,
three smashed Picasso men mark his sides.

          The trumpeter slouches, the rim of his hat
     tipped just enough to count the watching eyes.
          The rhythm player weeps, his bass a chronic load.

     The singer leans back, nothing to be but happy.
The intersection will always cheer.
                    The smile left after death

               is the only one
                    not facing death down.

Diary: 35th Birthday

The dream had to do with suspension, hanging,
   and now the alarm sounds—the groped-for light
     displaying the things the day must keep whole.

Winning is not promised. Just two days ago,
   I angled sharp scissors to cut the cardboard
     from a packet of shirts I drove downtown to buy

and sliced through the top one, the narrow space
   hoisted open with two fingers not wide enough
     for the blade to coast through. Shirts are fragile

and so are skin, love, memory, 35 years lived
   no more than 35 aimed with caution. Even today,
     Tuesday, I've only planned to be part daring,

coffee brewed at the usual time and shoes laid out
   for a dawn run to the gym. Someone else is up now,
     his lamp on and off in a window across the complex,

and as he locks the door hastily and rests his hand
   on the rail's spine trotting downstairs, I tell myself
     that he and I know the same things this morning:

his widow's peak and stubble caught by the street lamp
   pointing to 34, at least. As he checks his watch
     and pushes back a yawn, he passes a step too close

to the missing section of the chain-link fence
   with the ditch down the concrete slope behind it.
     Two months now and still no one has scaled

the gray decline to fetch the wrinkled twenty
   that sits at the bottom, the hard steepness and lack
     of a handrail apparently warnings enough.

Perhaps his conscience recalls the scene, a ditch
   like this one passed by for school years ago,
      a larger hand clutching his fingers tighter

as he leaned to glimpse the candy at the bottom.
   You have to stay where I can see you, she told him,
      steered him to where gravity was tamer. At 35,

we would like to say that the grips are our own,
   but the day fills with so many mothers' hands:
      Cetaphil for skin, yield signs, doctor's orders.

Tuesday now and we will take the bus again,
   its door sighing open by the curb like always.
      It will collect us, intact, and snap tightly to ride.

What We're Sure Of

1.

The poet whose grandfather died a week ago hugs me
and presses his card on the dim sum table to assure me
that all orders today are on him. For twenty minutes, longer,
he asks for nothing but stories—his arms folded on the table
and head tilted forward as though attention, rapt focus,
will buy some grace needed for later. My forced punchlines
finally exhausted, he sighs, tearful, and shakes his head.
Everything he knew is gone, he says. We picture memories, jokes,
hard-won lessons slipping away. Earth takes the body
and heaven may admit the soul, but does the mind side
with dust or ascension? Perhaps it floats in the middle,
the leavings of gray matter swirling over tables here
in between scents and steam. *Gone*, for us, may just mean
unreadable, too far for a voice or pen to set in code.
So many others passed today, time and again, and each
freeing of memory may have made the air thicker—
the sun squeezing its way through clusters of particles
and *there* weighing just barely more on each shoulder.
Did creation exist before we learned to imagine it?
How slighter was the world before we gave it names?

2.

Home to prepare for tutoring and I'm relieved that knowledge
is back in its physical bounds: the wooden CD case that I bought
as a child with the discs stacked in chronological order, creased
books on the shelf nearby holding the stories behind each song.
I am glad everything is in its place, but today the spines linger
like unanswered telephones, no incentive to power the speakers
or stretch to reach the top shelf when the gray matter recalls
so much. Even still, I have my old self to thank: the 12-year-old
who raced through homework, thrilled at the blank canvas
of an open hour and bent to listen on repeat to Bob Dylan
sing "A Hard Rain's A-Gonna Fall," each throaty phrase
and connection to the Cold War era adding to the stockpile
of what could someday be cashed in. This week, the U.S.
has mended walls with Cuba. *Fifty years coming*, some say.
The iron curtain looms elsewhere and we still have the tunes for it.
Meanwhile, rain keeps falling—on the road this morning,
I watched a woman huddle with her cart at the bus stop
while a plastic bucket gathered drops beside her. Each cupful
will have its use, laundry or wipes or a boiling mug of tea,
a source to ration; our luck determines what we learn from rain.

3.

At school now and the girl assigned to me laughs, Mark Twain
the white light on her Kindle and even the sober footnotes
close enough to be funny. They call her an English-learner
but that word applies to all of us, the definitions we gather
and pass to others never inventions of our own. She pauses
at *sever*, the cousin of *severe*, and I sketch a flailing hand cleaved
from the arm where it once belonged. *If you sever a hand*, I say,
you have a severe injury. She smiles, tugs a sleeve over her fingers.
Severe, like serious? Like serious, yes, and in no time,
we'll both be serious again—this knowledge we carry a talisman
that does nothing on its own, a ticket merely to buy the food
our stomachs cry for, an incantation against war and the storms
that hammer on our roofs. So many things out to dissolve us!
For what it's worth, we can classify them. The bell rings
and she jots *sever* in her binder, bows on her way to the door.
One more word today, a new prize weightless and hidden,
another piece of the trove assembled a blessing at a time.

Interview with the Songwriter

At the outdoor table, we write a night walk together.
   This is our project: myself the journalist on deadline
     and he the artist on the charts, this campus that inspired

his new song our halfway point to meet. My notepad spreads
   in front of me and I ask about the night walk. *Does it start
     here at the café?* Between sips from the flask, grinning, he tells

the tale of freshman year, his route back to the dorm
   after waiting tables, the window where he paused, night
     after night, to stare at the girl's silhouette, the drapes open

just an inch in the middle. *Even the moonlight risked peeking,*
   I jot down, then show him. We laugh. For half an hour, we
     have capped each other's sentences, fleshed out the night walk

with what words can evoke: a moon behind tree branches
   and smoke from an unseen joint, lyrics quoted from memory
     from Cream, Paul Simon, the education we each honed

in bookstores and hours by the radio. Had we met at 19,
   20 even, this night walk would not be a story but a song—
     our table in the dorm strewn with coffee cups, liner notes,

chords spun until dawn into a recorder's light. This year,
   the year after, is there time for sudden friendship? The talks
     come timed now, both of us with rings and planners, a text

on his phone cutting the hour short. He flashes the baby's
   picture, scatters tour schedule cards. *If you want to see the dorm,*
     he says, *it's the second on the right.* And he goes. I stay, left

    with what so many days amount to: a notepad scrawled
        with facts, two quotes, a promise to make no errors. There is
            barely time to linger, but with minutes, I take his night walk—

a day walk this time, all the drapes wide open. In one window,
    a girl plucks her guitar. In another, three boys laugh, their books
        strewn untouched, the sound of slow time and loved rapport.

Arboretum

Perched on one palm's strength, her knees dodging mud,
she jabs her stick and corrects the stream's defiance.

With her prodding, the rocks inch toward single file,
each shift jolting the current, muting its song.

Behind, her father pockets the life of Amelia Earhart,
their story for tonight. The book, he always chooses.

When they turn the globe at bedtime, as he knows they will,
what will she ask to find? The flight from Honolulu

may thrill her the most: the first pilot, woman or not,
to fly from Hawaii to the mainland, the black dot for Oakland

neat and round proclaiming the finish line. On the globe,
Howland Island hides unlabeled, too small for a finger's descent.

This is achievement, he practices mouthing already.
Her dolls wait at home, the one with the smudge thrown out.

It is the exploring, the perfect landings never promised.
For now, the riverbanks declare the moment's task.

Her stick too thin, she stretches to pull the thickest one
from the bottom, steels her wrist, gouges weeds aside.

Was the flow wrong before? She never stops to explain,
but her stick will not drop until it courses right.

As the stones give way, the surface flattens, calms,
each twist on the ground changing the sky's compliant shape.

To Rachanee, Laguna Beach, Jan. 1

Another holidays over and we've asked for less
than we've given away, the alarm's cold chime
waking us to our trusted inventory
of walls, ceiling, slotted sunlight.

To meet the new year, we drive to the streets
where our salaries would never buy a home
and slide six quarters—the year's first price—
into the meter a block from the beach.

Lace fingers, again, and let's enjoy
what is never given to us for keeps:
heaven, the absolute, whatever we name it
mirrored on the surface between wakes and buoys,

the robin's-egg sky that almost dissolves
past the water's edge on bleary days
now bold and separate, presiding master-like
over its more breakable half.

We are one day—always a day, not a year—
closer to broken, our bodies counting
toward an end whose only secret is time and place.
If we are lucky, someday, we will plan our letting go,

but this year is marked for holding what we can.
On the concrete steps, you choose the best angle,
touch your head to mine, click the iPhone camera.
With quarters, we will adore this sky later.

The responsibilities, stored at home, will wait.
How hard do we work to play at pausing time?
We thrive on boundaries pushed just enough,
our bliss bought with coins set aside.

One Word

He knows too few words in English
but his title at the top of the page, underlined twice,
points out his favorite: *heaven*.

On the more rickety of the wooden chairs
on the rickety planks of the porch next door,
he sits back-straight in the sun, lets heaven

spill in between the neighbors' jacarandas
and the ice cream truck he urges the kids to chase.
"When I was their age, that was heaven,"

he says, snapping his fingers to the bells,
and his tutor in the better chair, the much younger girl,
gives thumbs-up at the grammar. Their topic is heaven

and his deadline is next Monday, or Tuesday, no rush,
this letter to the local bishop intended
to make his case for confirmation. If heaven

were at stake with this letter, it would take a priest,
not a high school girl, to proof it to perfection,
but he seeks a different sort of heaven

on these three pages stacked to look like one—
these three eased, not torn, from the binder.
The essay, in a word, says: *I deserve heaven*,

or at least it will—the first line still eludes them.
Uncrumpling her own page, the girl suggests
that he make a cluster, write HEAVEN

large in the center and connect the words
that come to mind. All right, then: He twirls his pen
and writes *cars, girls, Selena*, then quotes: "Thank heaven

for 7-Eleven." They chuckle. "You think that's true?"
he asks, pointing a plumbing-scarred finger
above the trees to what must be heaven

and drawing a jagged line down, past the roofs,
to the market on the corner. "Probably not," he sighs.
With more words, he would say that we've gotten heaven

wrong, that the stars we see are only
the discards, the abandoned ones just bright enough
to evoke with metaphors and headlights, true heaven

a light beyond our corneas, a truth beyond
the words we inscribe. But the unknown is far off now
and today offers its own grace: the makeshift heaven

of a task completed, 500 right words in order
and a neat staple, the seal, in the upper left.
He shrugs, writes the first line: "I want to go to heaven."

To the Student Still Without
a First Draft Tuesday Morning

If you waste your time, I will waste mine better.
　　The weekend's exhausted and here we are again,
　　　　a two-day break usually, but this time it's three—
　　　　　　I count the days, and, oh, I know

you count them too, your insipid account
　　of what you did on Memorial Day weekend
　　　　summed up in three half-giggling words:
　　　　　　played video games. Yes, I remember those,

and unless my traumatic memories lie,
　　they involve plenty of losing: the little spaceship
　　　　exploding, again and again, only to be cued
　　　　　　back to life by a thumb's distracted tap.

Fingers ready, then! Let's restart the level
　　that we did last week. Unless you surprise me—
　　　　and miracles happen; that was the message
　　　　　　of the poem we read Friday—we will meet

at period's end with your page still empty,
　　your seatmate's phone (for I've confiscated yours)
　　　　more gripping than the rights of English women
　　　　　　during Austen's time. Wednesday, a stunner!

The TV will have stayed off, but your parents
　　will have threatened you with lack of dinner
　　　　or something unspeakable if you did homework
　　　　　　rather than clean your sister's dolls. Thursday,

after I've left two voicemails to discuss
　　your grade with your parents—or your sister,
　　　　close enough—you will slump into class,
　　　　　　your backpack slimmer than usual.

I accidentally threw everything out, you'll say,
   your line from last week—we both loved that.
     If you waste your time, I will waste mine better,
       spend hours up late grading the scraps

you've thought enough to pass forward,
   insist that you haven't crammed the Hemingway
     we both know is inside of you too far deep
       for reclamation. But when I say

that my time-wasting skills trump yours,
   mark my words as more than bragging.
     Rather, consider this: After the long nights
       of youth toiling for the SAT and college,

after the letters and the applications,
   after graduation, grad school and paid-off debt,
     after the handshakes, after the interviews,
       after the credential program and 12-hour days,

after training, taxes, the move, the mortgage,
   a man can blow his time, as I do with you,
     stuck forever on one impassable level,
       and, rather than get calls home for it, get *paid*.

Out of Ideas

In the back row, he sits hunched again,
his arms tight to his stomach
sheathed by winter sleeves in May.
Before him, the blank lines on the page
stare back like wan, vacant eyes.

This classroom is a city
and he has locked off his own town in it:
one where nothing works but dusk and sunrise,
the washed-out backs of buildings
bouncing teacher's pleas, classmates' offers,
every desperate sound into an echo.

What does he love
in this diminished home of his?
Is it the time to think,
the place to be unseen,
the safety of pacing the road unbothered?

Or is it the faith, the knowing
that if the locks finally tumble,
they will give to the right stranger,
the right astounding key?

II

Angels in Seven

December 27, 2014

1st

John! We've made it, you and I, twenty years
after our last sad phone call, this slow work evening
when my fingers punch your name into Google
and the screen whitens and flings it back for free—
your name, your security company on Manta
and a number listed. You've survived, and I have too!
Was I once naïve enough to think that you were
the only one at risk? Five years ago, in Portland, I stepped
off the curb and froze only when a stranger's voice
barked at me to watch the car, the wheels close enough
for heat as they swerved around the corner past me.
From the map, I can list more: the sprint over toll lanes
in West Virginia to barter with a driver for quarters
when my change ran out, the ride thumbed with strangers
to the campaign house in New Hampshire where we
tossed our bags on the floor, wallets vulnerable, and posted
candidate signs in the ice. Did your path turn out to be
the easier one? It is the small terrors, I know, that hound
us most, and perhaps the huge ones I feared for you—
drab apartments, debt, dollars scraped to buy milk—
were the ones you shrugged and smiled through. John,
we've made it, and the last time I heard your voice,
you sounded so near lost: June of 1994, the month
after eighth grade and weeks before high school split
our paths on schedule. I called to chat. Over the distance
of the phone, you sounded defensive, angry even,
your voice terse and hoarse and grunting short phrases

2nd

until a woman cried in the distance and you let the phone
clatter to a stop. You hoped to catch *Forrest Gump* before
it closed and I wished you luck—tickets, I knew, were
a treat for you. When I called weeks later, your line was out.
I never passed again by the cramped two-bedroom that I
visited once, the day your mother, on break between shifts
cleaning houses, uncrumpled a few bills to buy us Taco Bell
and you offered a worn stack of jigsaw puzzles for
the hour's entertainment. Instead of puzzles, we talked
about the Angels, our losing home team and the conversation
we plied week after week. Do you remember how it began?
The first day of seventh grade, our whole class terrified
in homeroom, I spotted you alone at the back table
and took the seat by you, my glasses and thin limbs
the things I knew to protect as I lugged my backpack
on one shoulder through a commons full of mirrors—
elementary school with its taunts escaped and my walk
still at an angle to everyone else's, my skin too gleaming
and words too precise. That first day meant shelter
and you offered it with your downcast stare, the bowl cut
that drooped with two hairs missed by the scissors,
arms spilled over the table, one draped on the other
as if stillness would be the best the day had to offer.
I knew you first as the best liar I'd met, our back table
livened for weeks by the tales about your heiress aunt,
your CIA brother, the haunted house your family bought
where you shut your eyes and still saw the devil. A lie

3rd

was no sin that fall when so much around us was fake:
David who threw rackets across the tennis court
when his teammates missed serves but hung his head
and took orders to behave from the smallest girl nearby,
the boys who demanded to know *Who's your backup?*
and never picked the fights they promised. When you
found I got the newspapers, a luxury not your own,
you started each morning with your giddy question—
Angels won, huh?—and sighed, long and troubled, when
I answered that they hadn't. Could I have lied?
For a smile, I might have, but I tore through
the sports page each morning to quell the same hunger,
a win for the home team a grace given to the world
though we both knew it wasn't given to us. The ballpark
was gift enough, one of 28 in the majors and erected
by chance a half hour from us. Over our homes,
over the school, it towered and gleamed, lit up with
the promise that greatness could happen here—
something celestial possible within the county limits
as we dodged the spit wads in the commons, passed up
our half-finished worksheets and prayed for a B.
Right now, the Angels have a new stadium and name
and the papers talk about how their huge payroll
is falling short of pennants. The team, its office staff
all seem hungry, hungry as we were twenty years ago.
Do you still follow the Angels, or did they leave us
both in time? This year Mike Trout is MVP, and though I

4th

saw him play last season, I don't remember him—any
home run or leaping catch imprinted less in my mind
than the strikeouts and bobbles we once memorized.
The second night of the '93 season, we went to the park
(your mother driving a friend's car), watched the Angels
move up 1 to 0 on Milwaukee and fall by a run in the ninth.
You kept score on a pad. At night, in my bedroom
with our sleeping bags stretched under the pennants,
you asked for whiteout, changed Rene Gonzales' flyout
with a runner on in the ninth to a two-run homer. *If we say
it happened, it did*, you insisted, twirling the pen.
That night, you started your notebook, every box score
that season written by hand with the play-by-plays.
If they won, it stayed untouched. If they lost, you
repaired it at the moment that went wrong:
the bobbled third-inning grounder snatched cleanly
and hurled for two outs, the line drive that died
at the warning track given enough wind to sail over.
Mornings in homeroom, the plastic radio I gifted you
having roared last night's game through static, you showed
your revisions, this perfect season our secret language that
we preserved with paper and nods. That summer, I tried
baseball for real, my one season of Little League
with a single base hit, two flies caught in practice.
Word got back to the locker room and the wet towels
flew harder, the team's loss last weekend recounted
with sadder errors each time. But my greatest games

5th

were the imagined ones, the hour before practice
with the field open, cleats on the lopsided mound,
fresh ball in hand hurled over the dusty plate in our
own perfect stadium, the empty bleachers roaring.
The glory was always to pitch, the rage that sent
a home run towering over the fence craved less
than the order of the ball snapping to the right spot
each time. Whoever threw precisely kept the score low,
the finesse of the bent ball decreeing which energies
would stay inside the park. John, did you
dream the same? Why did I never ask? Did you cast
yourself as the batter, Chili Davis with three runners on,
the unbelievable muscles pulsing to smash a drive
past the fence, the outstretched glove, fireworks bursting
like a benediction? Were you the fast center fielder,
Chad Curtis riding his 5'10" frame to the warning track,
a gasp as you stole the ball back in? I only remember
your sharpness, the smack of your palm on the table
when you displayed the notebook after the last game
in October, the word *UNDEFEATED!!!* scrawled
in capitals on the cover. We high-fived and laughed.
And then the off-season came, our best sanctuary
the track behind the portable classrooms, lunchtime
spent wandering around the loop as if walking
could scrape off school itself. That year, you inched
to a quiet place, the lies abandoned and your fingers
picking crumbs from your lunch tray, no notebook for '94.

6th

With your grades, you missed the class trip. I wandered
the theme park alone. The last day, you shook my hand.
Take care of yourself, you told me. From there, the ascent:
baseball cards given away, four years at the career center,
college, the newsroom, flights to England, two more
newsrooms, red-eyes, the longed-at map. And this evening
now, awaiting a source's email, I punch your name
into Google, stare at the number, breathe out and call.
You answer firmly, a stoic voice the right assurance
from a security guard on the phone. I give my name.
You chortle back. Yes, you're fine; yes, you made it
through high school, college unfinished but on your feet
without much debt. Married two years, newborn son,
wife has a bachelor's, business good. The strangers call
daily and smile when they see you, your uniform and car
the signs that their night will stay controlled. *Twenty years,*
you declare, fingers scratching your chin stubble.
Why this call now, tonight? The best I can say, John,
is that I am charmed by escapes now, each week flashing
with a reminder of what we shed—childhood feuds
mended on Facebook, the neighbors' son unloading toys
and rising at dawn to swim, Tim Salmon even bowing
his head at the prayer breakfast where he praised God
and set the ballpark in the past. If the park can go free,
then let our dreamed one go too. Let the wind give out,
the long drives finally fade! Forgive the bad hops, the errors!
The sky without fireworks, the things we couldn't will to win!

7th

I would say all of this but my tongue defies it, answers
only: *We've made it. Take care of yourself tonight.*
Eight o'clock and the shift beckons. You must run now.
You'll call back, you promise, baby crying in the distance.
We hang up and I am still needed, the newsroom empty
but for the night editor watching me, late files not in,
unattended phones ringing, lights on, papers strewn.
I know we will have no next call, but I will never care.
This year is for parting and I release you one last time,
into grace and memory and the hope the map gives us,
the mount on corkboard with pins in the cities
and the stretches between where we dream roads
for one another. I am short on them too, John,
the 30th pin stuck in this summer and 20 states to go,
the Great Plains open and New Orleans untouched,
any trip promising a step forward, a destination
bolder than here. And all I know to tell you is that
New Hampshire freezes, that traffic rushes in Portland
and West Virginia has steep turns; the tolls are steeper,
so we'll keep change at all times. We'll travel by day, too.
Let's always chase the light. In 2002, the Angels took
the World Series in seven games, John Lackey, the rookie,
starting the clincher and Darin Erstad catching the final fly.
Box score was 4 to 1, first matchup of wild cards,
San Francisco the loser, Troy Glaus named MVP.
I was out of the country and read the *Times* online.
Did you buy a paper then? Could you miss the news?

III

Men at the Hotel Pool

With a single pale look, the boy casts them as judges.
    Naked but for wet trunks, he sets his glasses down
and shakes his wavy bangs back, his half-soft face
    revealing the bones that his skin will tighten to grip.

The tournament starts here and the course lies before him,
    by the tanned, sullen girl who flops on the recliner
and hasn't moved in an hour. With the bottles all open
    and the women—elsewhere—defined by doctor bills

and names, the man at the edge of the bar whips out
    a cigar from Havana. *Best smoke in the world says*
she looks at him, he mutters. *Five dollars says no*, another
    voice grunts back. Since the four of them sat down,

the boy has swum beside her, taken the recliner
    next to hers and pretended to read. Her shades
point skyward, hair and breasts splayed in the sun.
    Twelve or so, his chin just old enough

to dodge any comforting hand beneath it,
    he meanders toward the board now. This walk
they remember: too careful to be cocky, too smooth
    to watch the footing, eyes pink from chlorine

but no grimace from the sting. At the board's cliff,
    he stretches, fingertips slowly pressed together,
then heaves forward—blindly, they know—his form
    a perfect stiff line, the surface dashed, then still again.

When the girl sits up, the dollars change fingers.
    She furrows her brow, slides the shades on again.
The boy sits by her, pleased, this spot his undisputed,
    the reward for upsetting whatever odds there were.

Woman Next Door

The door yanked open first and left
like an overture that builds to her voice,

she appears with one foot out of the house,
the Fender bass resisting the dig of her fingertips

before she stalks out and heaves it onto the lawn,
turns to flip the bird and storms back in.

In a second, she's out again—her retreats and exits
as abrupt as a boxer's steady left, right, left.

Her flight takes her to the street corner lamp,
the crossroads where she pauses, red and pierced,

each direction gleaming with its late-day overture
of turn signals, vacancy signs. From here,

behind the window glass, what can we do?
There has been no crime, no blood, no struggle,

no name or shared history that would beseech us
to tell off the man, clear the guest room for her.

Our hospitality quails at the conditions we've set.
All we have left is our own inspection: our eyes

that drift to the living room and mark the corners
without guitars or amps, the books we've checked out

for each other, the hour's small talk priming the air.
Each morning, each morning, we wake unaware

of the things we've won without trying.

Day After New Year's

On the well-behaved days behind the complex gates,
any eyes can volunteer to play police.

This morning, the man in the ironed jacket
appoints himself in charge for a moment,

his slow sidelong gaze at the boys
who loitered too closely to the woman's garage

enough to send them sauntering off.
In an instant, it ends. Walking alone, he passes the girls

who kneel on a blanket beside the new Volvo
and stack their Legos: two boxes, not shared,

the pinks and blues like his sisters once hoarded
in the house on another block years ago.

He stops to watch. One girl glances, sees him,
the pulse that quivers through her face an instant review

of his dark jacket, anonymity, stare.
They leave the Legos in place, duck past the car.

The small one speaks to a shadow through the door.
The man walks on, faster, the neighborhood filled

with the remnants of last week—wreaths left out
for recycling, extensions, unplugged Santas.

The trimmed lawns, the thresholds lay down their rules.
This year will pay the same price for resolution as the last.

After His First Surgery

She swore to love all of him
but the lesion does not count.
If it is not him, what does she name it?
This dot of flesh will go
under the doctor's light,
a message to be relayed
like the paper that slaps the porch.

*

Whatever he clings to,
whatever they excise,
the body will stop working in time.
If this is God's plan,
they must be in awe of it.

*

On the mattress, by decree,
he watches her sideways.
Her wrist holds the mug steady,
her gray hairs just a glint of iron.
Today, this time,
he lies and she stands.
He changes the subject before deciding
if he would have them trade places.

*

The doctor urges *no exercise*
but they set their alarm for 5.
When it rings, they will resent it.
When their run is over,
they will love the sweat, the ache.

*

While he sleeps, she dusts off the attic box
and finds the stuffed cow
she slept with as a child.
In her hands, it shrinks into a ball
until the limbs and head
spring back with her release.
For now, this is the miracle.
The time is finite when the body
will reclaim its bounds each time.

Salvaged

The oldest says *Leave everything be*, but the others go to search
for what can be spirited out. As their parents huddle
with the estate lawyer in the kitchen, they squeeze past one another
to the front room—all the back ones requiring stepping

at an angle with their gnarled boxes and last century's papers.
At the end of the hall with the bulb shorted out, the floor
and walls swell to radiance, bright afternoon bathing the items
half-boxed: turntable, medals, china chipped in the case.

It's a coincidence, this arrangement, the house up a parching slope
built half a century back when the neighborhood settled
where it could—the front door by a planner's discretion opening
straight to the largest room without a foyer or hat rack—

but today the foundation seems to strain its calves to meet
the rays an instant sooner. The great-aunt has died now,
the great-uncle before her, and with each thing removed,
the room loses more to sunlight. At this time, is there a difference

between theft and assistance? The middle sister claims
the Jolson records, vinyl the rage at school and the covers perfect
for Instagram. The youngest pockets a teacup from the box
marked for storage, her sly gift the saving of a thing for use.

Ride Home

His mother's eyes without a mouth in the mirror,
he slouches, rain-drenched, loose like a doll.

The one prize from the fair, the stuffed red giraffe
that she shelled out to help him win, curls in his arm.

This outing was their secret, her red circle made
on the calendar this morning, a day marked for nothing else.

To break the silence after each wipe on the windshield,
she asks him to name his favorite part.

The ball toss, he mutters, his focus on the window.
He picks a hair off his crown, scowls, sets it back.

The ball toss will do. A favorite of any kind leaves
the day won, resolved, a label stuck on what is clear.

At home, they will ease back into the put-off questions,
the studied tact, three asleep in different rooms.

The man will take the giraffe's picture. The heater will start,
their shoes kicked off in a heap to dry together.

Over soup, they will say grace for what is second-rate—
thanks, like secrets, the art of leaving the right parts unsaid.

First Condo

The buyer takes it while we're on vacation.
Over attached documents at the library computer,
we read his name, apply signatures, leave for tea.

Some time while we drove the rocky coast
or stepped past pines to see the Atlantic,
he passed through with the Realtor—a structure

that meant one thing to us soon to be
cleaned and re-carpeted to mean something new
for him. We stayed in a friend's friend's cabin

this week, a structure like any; the returns
of attaching deep meaning have diminished more
for us each year. Still, the ease of this transaction,

even for fees, evokes a smiling time—when moves
were planned in private by older voices, behind doors,
our only task to pack and await the sign to go.

New Place

We've packed the heaviest things
in the back of the van
and so the fragile ones come first.

First bag opened: push pins,
the bright markers we stick after travels
into our map mounted on corkboard.

This city where we've moved
is too close to the last
to warrant a monument of its own.

When we cart in the map,
we will push the current pin deeper,
the crease on the matte its own celebration.

Mattress, sheets, three heavy bags follow.
One holds our toiletries,
and we call it a night.

The half-sleep to come will be like no other:
the rooms around us still a why-not,
blank walls, a space to test out dreams.

The next morning, we will muscle in boxes,
declare what is outside with the double-lock.
We will hug at our collective might.

Our Money's Worth

Saturday at the Honda dealer,
two more errands to go,
we park it for the last time
and wet a tissue to rub the stain
from the frayed plastic top of the key.

In a bright, hot office,
we smile wanly at the numbers:
200,000 miles without a breakdown
worth $1,500 when traded in.
As the woman explains the spreadsheet
(no bargain in the offing),

the frail man through the glass door
widens an eye to meet the headlamp
he steadies his thin rag to shine.
In our thirties now,
we have logged enough milestones
to know not to dwell on new ones,

and so when the woman sighs
Two hundred thousand without a breakdown,
we nod that, yes, the dealers served it well—
snow tires in Connecticut
and lubes on the desert drives,
no seam on the side mirror from the shop
after the hit-and-run at the curb.

A signature now, two hard handshakes
and we toast with bottled water
to what did not let us down—
no Jim or Luke or Pedro
here in factory clothes to thank in person,
luck the only name we can give
to what kept each wheel steady,
the brakes resilient and tight.

IV

Poems at the Station

> *there is time and hopefully*
> *a train*
> *—Lee Mallory*

6:57 a.m.

Outline of a white oak stretched
on the sidewalk by the depot—
this shadow stayed as the frontier
gave to concrete below it.

10:30 a.m.

Bony child on the cup
and two dollars clang in.
The world is broken
and fixed every instant.

1:18 p.m.

Overtime and the state team
sets at the 10-yard line.
Time called. A tear shed?
Even police crowd the TV.

4:03 p.m.

Feet move around
the unscratched lottery ticket.
Behind them the toddler
stomps twice on every crack.

7:15 p.m.

Composer's face on magazines
and three headsets play the concerto.
Every great thought
like a syringe into the universe.

11:59 p.m.

Obituary shows on
the front page through the dispenser.
One fewer set of ears
will recognize the whistle.

Departures

A smack of tide on the docking sail
    scatters drops over Fisherman's Wharf
          and Casey and I duck startled
       under the spray—

  this laughter a music that we have honed for 30 years,
    palms perched on each other's shoulders declaring
      If you get wet, I'll share your misery.

Some time between our birthdays, and he has a gift,
    this day as good as any for one more blessing:
sky watercolor blue and the wind tossing

whatever it catches up high,
  everything from the lurching sails

    to our stray strands of hair a reminder
that gravity claims only half our home.
          On the table, the notebook!

Here, his name on top of mine
  on the school project dated 18 years ago,

  these pages never meant for a museum
clean and preserved behind a stained plastic binder.
      Eighteen years ago

we sprawled in his living room,
  the photocopied pages of Emily Dickinson

  scattered on the rug as sun split the curtains.
    Safe in their alabaster chambers
                the first line read—

the soft seclusion of this image
    as welcoming as his parents' tract house,
  and I told myself then

    that these words would someday be a comfort:

a phrase rushed through my mind
      to halt whatever chaos time had started,
  a charm to set breath and sensation back

    to when everything was sure.

*

        This morning at the café,
      before the flight at 2:17,

  we trade notes on the unknowns,

our guesses about marriage and God and children
      the counter to the waves' unflagging rhythm.

  We could cast this notebook to the tide as well,
but through mercy we keep it,
                today a better day

    to let Earth do the dispensing.
  It will dispense with us too,
           by and by,

    and for now the diminishments
are their own discovery:

      my hair with its strips of gray
         that have stopped the grocery clerks from carding me,

  his laughter lines still marking the places
where the harder sarcasm ebbed with age,

    his height, so tall to make our hug an awkward stoop,
       that the years will always hold
          a head above mine.

                *

On the plane back from San Francisco
   and in my mind, everything is flying—

     this gift of transport from the inventors before us

   now feeding all our dreams of departing.
     In the photos in the dusty yearbooks
our classmates cluster side by side,

     and in the decades since
                we have all moved to the air:

     a thousand or more flights
   dispatching us where flights can go,
our texts and updates borne on invisible waves.

With the fake fears from high school
   now given way to real ones,

     even the sky should alert our suspicion,

   but the notion of flight still serves as promise.
Look outside the window now:
                not a rain cloud in sight

   and the green ball fields outshining the ghettos,

   the snow-packed mountains too jagged for skiing
     gripping the eyes as they grip the sun,

the simple distance of far enough
   turning so many of our dangers
            into beauty.

Park in Reykjavik, Iceland

The wind
        has snatched the Frisbee
                      and the boy

  scrambles into the bushes
                to catch it in flight

as though the ground
            would score a point
                      for touching it first.

In shorts, he slackens
            and bolts back straight

  to navigate the branches
           that cut him already.
                        When he throws

the Frisbee to the woman
            who left her purse half-spilled

  on the bench,
            the wind deflects it
                    and cues the race again.

    No one reads
             the newspaper that dances
                        across the square

by the flower garden,
            but there must be news
                        about wind somewhere:

    a typhoon that tore roofs
                      off the huts in Ghana

or a man who died of chill
                in the coldest capital.

   So often the elements
              give us hints
                        of what they're capable of;

if we stay whole
         through them,
                we call it bravery, sport.

   Today at the Blue Lagoon,
                    I watched two men wince

at the jagged rocks
             under the steaming surface

  but walk until the heat
             nearly blistered

  before the signs by the incline
                   that urged *No Entry*.

The edges too blunt
            to puncture skin
                     cause the feet not to turn

  but to step on boldly,
              and sometimes even blood—

a scar to keep—
         only tempts us
                to laugh off more.

  At the park now, the boy
             rolls his pant leg higher

to show his mark
    to the younger one beside him,
           this red jag

that will heal to pink
     the new trophy.
        The woman

  shakes her purse,
      shakes her head,
         no tissue in sight.

The wind,
   which started this,
       will fan the leg dry.

Housewarming, East Los Angeles

Someone across the patio calls the neighborhood *sketchy*
   and the woman at the far end, who has sipped her beer alone
      and tapped her throat to indicate where the operation

took her voice, hoists up a pad and pen and displays them
   like a magician with a handkerchief too thin to pack a dove.
      The few of us between conversations her audience, she starts

with the slim bones of the surroundings: rugged hill above
   the winding street that the parked cars shrink to one lane,
      stray dog slouched on the corner, a single balloon on the rail

that indicates a party at this house up the crooked steps.
   On the patio before the open gate that she sketches without
      the padlock dangling, the crowd half-covers the blank space.

The pen rests for a minute and she shows us our ritual:
   this whiteness marked only by the outlines of gathering,
      the compulsion to touch and not drink alone. Without words

or faces to tell our stories, do the lines show if we celebrate
   or mourn? The new homeowners toast with their margaritas,
      the man's fingers spreading to show the ring to her parents,

but joy and grief make their own congregations—a circle just
   as tight around the landlady who holds her late mother's Polaroid
      and nods eagerly at condolences with her tears having dried.

All that unites us are our neat survivals, this touch of sky
   and nearness with friends what we run to at any hour
      when a room is not enough—the bottles that fizz one by one

an incantation against silence, solitude. Our society captured
   now on her pad, the artist fills in its boundaries. At the curb below
      the steps, three men saunter by and watch, their faces too distant

to read but their gait slowing to signal thirst. Down the block,
   two boys set bottles on the fence and let fly with a slingshot,
      one stone per turn, the game won by what is broken just right.

Bonfire at Cape Cod with Marge Piercy's Workshop

No one has brought a first draft. On this smooth strip of beach
that someone pocked with a shovel, two feet deep and wide,

we use the ordinary items for kindling: the same front page
of the *Cape Cod Times* wadded again and again to fit

the gaps between logs, thin planks with nails still stuck out
and curled. When the last embers burn out, only the nails

will keep their shape—our materials outlived by what almost
held them together. For the last week around the table,

we've dissected our scraps. The words worth keeping
have gone to folders and the rest to piles, compost or recycling,

whatever fate we assign to our thoughts that will not survive
the year. The useful things will still serve us. The binders

that held our worst drafts will hold our best someday,
the pens retain their ink, the tide continue to crash

even if all we can write is that it crashes a lot, loudly,
a rhythm we read too much into. Here on the sand,

the work week done, we are content to watch the show.
The flames toss up patterns, flash, then withdraw them;

the sky pulls its nightly trick, wrings red and pink from blue.
When it darkens, we head back. With our directions,

in separate cars, we navigate the roads without names,
finesse the sharp turns, one hand ready on the brights

until we return to the cabins, the locked doors and luggage,
our retreat to the things we know better than to lose.

Crossing, Harpers Ferry

Ten minutes since the gas station and the map is lost already,
      let loose for an instant by distracted fingers and swept
           by the breeze across shoe tops half a block down.

To make our maps was achievement, centuries of fine hands
      setting the lines in place before the cameras proved
           what we had guessed correctly, but with

the rivers so close, it is as good a time as any to surrender
      the markings that pointed us here. In the skeleton
           of this Civil War town where caretakers

work to preserve the bones, we celebrate the age of what
      can be traced to a year: John Brown's fort marked
           with a mounted placard while the gift shops

declare that uprisings here are through. Today's sightseeing
      begins in the town, but the road consummates in what
           thrills beyond it: two metal railings that intersect

as the Shenandoah and Potomac rage together. What we find
      charming past this point is up to us, the harsh churn
           of mud and branches, day and night, marking

the side where might has its way. Do we defeat the current only
      by staying out of its path? Up the hill, the aged hotels
           sit above overflow's reach, while the foot bridges

lure us on trips that borderlines proclaim. On this bank, our feet
      touch West Virginia; a walk across, an ease off the handrail,
           and we gaze back from Maryland. Even when

    the water separates them for us, we know the states count
            for something—years of construction and Constitution
                    firming the feats we call our own. This town

    stands, ready for evening, benches poised toward the river. For $1
            at the gift shop, a map offers the safe routes back, our
                    settlements the stops between what can only flow.

Virginia Museum of Fine Arts

Thirty-sixth summer and the milestones
      line up to step another year back—

27 now since the month before school
when I sprang from bed at dawn
      and tore from screen door to yard and back

      as if motion
           could stretch late August further,

18 since the first car beckoned
   and the nights blossomed to night drives,
      myself and my reflection high-school thin

      seeking absolution from the radio.
By now, contentment having slipped enough
      that I know it is never lost for good,

    I have taught myself to avoid the task
of running to recover it.
                This Tuesday

on vacation, passing the ones headed to work,
   I let my reflection in the windows
      smile itself out of sight—

   this morning at the museum a nice excursion
and this framed Pollock worth a minute's look,
   a dinner at the Mexican café treat enough

      as a night's respite from doing dishes.
The rental car will time out soon
                and the plane

return home, the dishes fill the counter
         to mark another day outlived.

The joy is not in the holding but in
         the slipping through the fingers,

                  and each year reminds us
                           that what calms us most
                  are the things we never lacked:

   the bleacher shadows' stretch at the park
      on a walk
                  after the pickup game is over,

the alarm's reminder that the last day
         stopped unfinished,

         the water filter in the kitchen
      that drips barely audibly,
                  hour after hour,

         our incredible source through the night.

Alaska Airlines Nonstop to LAX

Before the planes turned to ram the Twin Towers,
they hummed in a straight line just like this—
an achievement always to stay calm facing forward
and most remarkable when wings and circuits
keep us suspended over a space too vast
to be even called a drop. The sky that radiates blue
from below turns to nothing when looked at
from above, but here on board, we cling
to the somethings we have: water closer to us
in the plastic bottles than in the particles
of clouds, *American Hustle* on the in-flight movie
catching more stares than the mountaintops
that will never bounce light just this way again.
The story goes that even the astronauts
played Hank Williams on Apollo 13
until the batteries died, and perhaps in the face
of the possible fireball, all we know is the language
we packed from home. Given one more minute,
how many of us would opt for last words,
some grand phrase to resolve up high
what was left unfinished miles below?
The fullest circle would be to go in silence,
to let sky outlive the word for sky
and thrill one last time to what light and color gave—
the outpost of ground and expansion of blue
and the promise that thoughts could help us climb.

Acknowledgments

Thanks to the editors of the following publications in which these poems first appeared, sometimes in slightly different versions:

American Mustard: "The Chicago Window Washer Lets His Soap Paintings Stay"
Cadence Collective: "One Word," "Woman Next Door," "Day After New Year's"
Muddy River Poetry Review: "Arboretum," "Housewarming, East Los Angeles"
Poetry Quarterly: "Bonfire at Cape Cod with Marge Piercy's Workshop"
Zocalo Public Square: "Park in Reykjavik, Iceland"

This book would not have been possible without the assistance and dedication of two workshops: the Laguna Poets, who meet every month in Laguna Beach, California, and Marge Piercy's annual summer writing retreat in Cape Cod, Massachusetts. Additional thanks to Irena Praitis, Ricki Mandeville and Gail Newman, who read the manuscript as a whole and gave valuable feedback.

Thanks to Susan Davis ("The Season Begins in a Waiting Room," *I Was Building Up to Something*, Moon Tide Press, 2011) and Lee Mallory ("Order," *Now and Then*, Moon Tide Press, 2009) for permission to use their epigraphs.

As always, thanks to my family—and to Rachanee, for so much.

As this book prepared to go to press, we received news of the untimely death of Amanda Walzer, who helped to spearhead the Visiting Writer program at Fullerton College. Amanda was a great supporter of Moon Tide Press over the years and dedicated a significant part of her life to bringing talented poets together with students who were eager to learn. Her passing comes as a shock to all, and our thoughts and prayers go out to her family.

About the Author

Michael Miller is the cofounder of Moon Tide Press and the author of *College Town* (Tebot Bach, 2010) and *The First Thing Mastered* (Tebot Bach, 2013). A longtime journalist, he has written for the *Los Angeles Times* and other publications and won a 2014 Orange County Press Club award for his story on poets Lee Mallory and Charles Bukowski. He and his wife, Rachanee Srisavasdi, live in Los Angeles.

www.ingramcontent.com/pod-product-compliance
Lightning Source LLC
Chambersburg PA
CBHW031211090426
42736CB00009B/871